50 Snowy House Dishes

By: Kelly Johnson

Table of Contents

- Chicken Pot Pie
- Beef Stew
- Baked Mac and Cheese
- Hot Chocolate
- Winter Squash Soup
- Shepherd's Pie
- Slow Cooker Chili
- Roasted Root Vegetables
- Beef Wellington
- Baked Ziti
- French Onion Soup
- Pot Roast
- Garlic Mashed Potatoes
- Spaghetti Carbonara
- Creamy Tomato Soup
- Chicken and Rice Casserole
- Roasted Chicken with Herbs
- Eggplant Parmesan
- Stuffed Mushrooms

- Grilled Cheese Sandwich
- Butternut Squash Risotto
- Chicken Noodle Soup
- Cinnamon Rolls
- Sticky Toffee Pudding
- Baked Sweet Potatoes
- Mushroom Risotto
- Roasted Brussels Sprouts
- Salmon Chowder
- Warm Spinach and Bacon Salad
- Meatloaf
- Potato Leek Soup
- Baked Apple Crisp
- Spiced Pear Tart
- Lamb Stew
- Chicken Alfredo
- Cauliflower Gratin
- Pulled Pork Sandwiches
- Risotto with Winter Greens
- Potato Gratin
- Lemon Bread Pudding

- Apple and Cranberry Sauce
- Mulled Wine
- Goulash
- Baked Brie with Jam
- Chocolate Lava Cake
- Eggnog
- Roasted Chestnuts
- Caramelized Onion Soup
- Pumpkin Bread
- Snowball Cookies

Chicken Pot Pie

Ingredients:

- 1 lb cooked chicken, shredded
- 1 cup frozen peas and carrots
- 1/2 cup chopped onions
- 1/2 cup celery, chopped
- 1/4 cup flour
- 2 cups chicken broth
- 1 cup milk
- 1 tsp garlic powder
- 1 tsp thyme
- 1 package refrigerated pie crusts
- Salt and pepper to taste

Instructions:

1. Preheat the oven to 425°F (220°C).
2. In a large skillet, sauté onions and celery until softened. Add peas, carrots, garlic powder, and thyme, and cook for another 2 minutes.
3. Stir in flour and cook for 1 minute. Slowly add chicken broth and milk, stirring constantly until thickened.
4. Add the shredded chicken and season with salt and pepper.
5. Roll out one pie crust and place it in a pie dish. Pour the chicken mixture into the pie crust. Top with the second pie crust and crimp the edges.
6. Cut slits in the top to allow steam to escape. Bake for 30-35 minutes, until golden brown.

Beef Stew

Ingredients:

- 2 lbs beef stew meat, cubed
- 4 medium potatoes, cubed
- 2 carrots, sliced
- 1 onion, chopped
- 2 garlic cloves, minced
- 4 cups beef broth
- 1/2 cup red wine (optional)
- 1 tbsp tomato paste
- 2 tsp thyme
- 2 bay leaves
- Salt and pepper to taste

Instructions:

1. In a large pot, brown the beef stew meat in a little oil over medium heat. Remove the beef and set aside.
2. In the same pot, sauté onions and garlic until softened. Add tomato paste and cook for 1 minute.
3. Add beef broth, wine (if using), thyme, bay leaves, and the browned beef. Bring to a simmer.
4. Add potatoes and carrots. Cover and cook for 1-1.5 hours, or until beef is tender and vegetables are cooked.
5. Season with salt and pepper to taste before serving.

Baked Mac and Cheese

Ingredients:

- 1 lb elbow macaroni
- 2 cups shredded cheddar cheese
- 1 cup grated Parmesan cheese
- 2 cups milk
- 1/4 cup butter
- 1/4 cup flour
- 1 tsp mustard powder
- 1/2 tsp garlic powder
- Salt and pepper to taste

Instructions:

1. Preheat the oven to 350°F (175°C).
2. Cook the macaroni according to package instructions and drain.
3. In a large saucepan, melt butter over medium heat. Whisk in flour and cook for 1 minute.
4. Slowly add the milk, whisking constantly until the sauce thickens. Stir in mustard powder, garlic powder, cheddar cheese, and Parmesan.
5. Combine the cheese sauce with the cooked macaroni and season with salt and pepper.
6. Transfer to a greased baking dish, top with extra cheese, and bake for 20 minutes, until golden and bubbly.

Hot Chocolate

Ingredients:

- 2 cups milk
- 1/2 cup heavy cream
- 1/2 cup chocolate chips or cocoa powder
- 2 tbsp sugar (optional)
- 1 tsp vanilla extract

Instructions:

1. In a saucepan, heat the milk and cream over medium heat until warm.
2. Stir in chocolate chips or cocoa powder and sugar, whisking until smooth and heated through.
3. Remove from heat and add vanilla extract.
4. Serve hot, topped with whipped cream or marshmallows, if desired.

Winter Squash Soup

Ingredients:

- 1 medium butternut squash, peeled and cubed
- 1 onion, chopped
- 2 garlic cloves, minced
- 4 cups vegetable or chicken broth
- 1/2 cup coconut milk (optional)
- 1 tsp ground ginger
- 1/2 tsp cinnamon
- Salt and pepper to taste

Instructions:

1. In a large pot, sauté onions and garlic until softened.
2. Add the cubed squash, broth, ginger, and cinnamon. Bring to a boil.
3. Lower the heat and simmer for 20-30 minutes, or until the squash is tender.
4. Use an immersion blender to blend the soup until smooth. Add coconut milk for creaminess, if desired.
5. Season with salt and pepper, and serve warm.

Shepherd's Pie

Ingredients:

- 1 lb ground beef or lamb
- 1 onion, chopped
- 2 carrots, chopped
- 1 cup peas
- 2 tbsp tomato paste
- 1 cup beef broth
- 4 large potatoes, peeled and mashed
- 1/4 cup butter
- 1/4 cup milk
- Salt and pepper to taste

Instructions:

1. Preheat the oven to 375°F (190°C).
2. In a skillet, brown the ground meat with onions and carrots. Stir in tomato paste and cook for 1 minute.
3. Add beef broth and simmer for 10 minutes until thickened. Stir in peas.
4. In a separate bowl, mash the potatoes with butter, milk, salt, and pepper.
5. Transfer the meat mixture to a baking dish and top with the mashed potatoes.
6. Bake for 20 minutes, or until the top is golden brown.

Slow Cooker Chili

Ingredients:

- 1 lb ground beef or turkey
- 1 onion, chopped
- 1 bell pepper, chopped
- 2 garlic cloves, minced
- 1 can (14.5 oz) diced tomatoes
- 1 can (15 oz) kidney beans, drained
- 1 can (15 oz) black beans, drained
- 2 tbsp chili powder
- 1 tsp cumin
- 1/2 tsp paprika
- Salt and pepper to taste

Instructions:

1. Brown the ground meat in a skillet over medium heat, then transfer it to the slow cooker.
2. Add the chopped onion, bell pepper, garlic, diced tomatoes, beans, chili powder, cumin, and paprika to the slow cooker.
3. Stir to combine, cover, and cook on low for 6-8 hours or high for 3-4 hours.
4. Season with salt and pepper before serving.

Roasted Root Vegetables

Ingredients:

- 2 large carrots, peeled and chopped
- 2 parsnips, peeled and chopped
- 2 sweet potatoes, peeled and chopped
- 1 tbsp olive oil
- 1 tsp rosemary
- Salt and pepper to taste

Instructions:

1. Preheat the oven to 400°F (200°C).
2. Toss the vegetables with olive oil, rosemary, salt, and pepper.
3. Spread them out on a baking sheet in a single layer.
4. Roast for 25-30 minutes, or until tender and lightly browned, stirring halfway through.

Beef Wellington

Ingredients:

- 2 lb beef tenderloin
- 1 lb mushrooms, chopped
- 2 tbsp Dijon mustard
- 1 sheet puff pastry
- 1 egg, beaten
- Salt and pepper to taste

Instructions:

1. Preheat the oven to 400°F (200°C).
2. Sear the beef tenderloin in a hot pan with salt and pepper. Remove and brush with Dijon mustard.
3. In the same pan, cook the mushrooms until all moisture has evaporated.
4. Roll out the puff pastry, place the beef on it, and cover with the mushroom mixture. Wrap the beef with the pastry and seal edges.
5. Brush with beaten egg and bake for 25-30 minutes until golden. Let rest for 10 minutes before slicing.

Baked Ziti

Ingredients:

- 1 lb ziti pasta
- 2 cups marinara sauce
- 2 cups ricotta cheese
- 2 cups mozzarella cheese, shredded
- 1/4 cup Parmesan cheese
- 1 egg, beaten
- 1 tbsp basil, chopped

Instructions:

1. Preheat the oven to 375°F (190°C).
2. Cook the pasta according to package instructions, drain.
3. Mix the cooked pasta with marinara sauce, ricotta, mozzarella, Parmesan, egg, and basil.
4. Pour into a greased baking dish and top with extra mozzarella.
5. Bake for 25 minutes, or until bubbly and golden.

French Onion Soup

Ingredients:

- 4 large onions, thinly sliced
- 2 tbsp butter
- 1 tbsp olive oil
- 1 tsp sugar
- 2 cloves garlic, minced
- 1/4 cup dry white wine
- 6 cups beef broth
- 1 tsp thyme
- 1 bay leaf
- Salt and pepper to taste
- Baguette slices, toasted
- 1 1/2 cups Gruyère cheese, shredded

Instructions:

1. In a large pot, melt butter and olive oil over medium heat. Add onions and sugar. Cook, stirring occasionally, for 30-40 minutes until onions are caramelized and golden brown.
2. Add garlic and cook for 1 minute. Pour in wine and let it reduce for 3 minutes.
3. Add beef broth, thyme, bay leaf, salt, and pepper. Bring to a simmer and cook for 20 minutes.
4. Ladle the soup into oven-safe bowls, top with toasted baguette slices, and sprinkle with Gruyère cheese.
5. Place under the broiler for 3-5 minutes, until the cheese is melted and bubbly.

Pot Roast

Ingredients:

- 3-4 lb beef chuck roast
- 4 large carrots, peeled and chopped
- 4 potatoes, peeled and chopped
- 1 onion, quartered
- 3 cloves garlic, minced
- 2 cups beef broth
- 1/4 cup red wine (optional)
- 2 tbsp tomato paste
- 2 tsp rosemary
- 1 tsp thyme
- Salt and pepper to taste

Instructions:

1. Preheat the oven to 325°F (165°C).
2. In a large oven-safe pot, sear the beef roast on all sides over medium-high heat.
3. Remove the beef and set it aside. In the same pot, sauté onions, garlic, and tomato paste for 3 minutes.
4. Add beef broth, red wine (if using), rosemary, thyme, salt, and pepper. Stir to combine.
5. Return the roast to the pot and surround it with carrots and potatoes.
6. Cover and roast for 3-4 hours, until the meat is tender and easily shreds.

Garlic Mashed Potatoes

Ingredients:

- 2 lbs potatoes, peeled and chopped
- 4 cloves garlic, minced
- 1/2 cup butter
- 1/2 cup milk
- Salt and pepper to taste

Instructions:

1. Boil the potatoes in salted water until tender, about 15 minutes.
2. While the potatoes are cooking, melt butter in a pan and sauté garlic for 1 minute.
3. Drain the potatoes and return them to the pot.
4. Mash the potatoes with the butter and garlic mixture, adding milk until smooth.
5. Season with salt and pepper to taste.

Spaghetti Carbonara

Ingredients:

- 12 oz spaghetti
- 4 oz pancetta or bacon, diced
- 2 eggs
- 1/2 cup Parmesan cheese, grated
- 1/4 cup heavy cream (optional)
- 2 cloves garlic, minced
- Salt and pepper to taste

Instructions:

1. Cook the spaghetti according to package instructions, reserving 1/2 cup of pasta water.
2. In a large pan, cook pancetta or bacon until crispy. Add garlic and cook for 1 minute.
3. In a bowl, whisk together eggs, Parmesan, heavy cream (if using), and a pinch of pepper.
4. Add the cooked pasta to the pan with pancetta and toss to combine. Remove from heat and quickly stir in the egg mixture, adding pasta water to create a creamy sauce.
5. Serve with extra Parmesan and black pepper.

Creamy Tomato Soup

Ingredients:

- 2 tbsp olive oil
- 1 onion, chopped
- 2 garlic cloves, minced
- 2 cans (14.5 oz each) diced tomatoes
- 1 cup vegetable broth
- 1/2 cup heavy cream
- 1 tsp sugar
- Salt and pepper to taste

Instructions:

1. Heat olive oil in a pot over medium heat. Sauté onions and garlic for 5 minutes until softened.
2. Add the diced tomatoes, vegetable broth, sugar, salt, and pepper. Bring to a simmer and cook for 15 minutes.
3. Use an immersion blender to blend the soup until smooth. Stir in heavy cream and cook for an additional 5 minutes.
4. Adjust seasoning with salt and pepper and serve warm.

Chicken and Rice Casserole

Ingredients:

- 2 cups cooked chicken, shredded
- 1 cup uncooked rice
- 1 can (10.5 oz) cream of mushroom soup
- 1/2 cup milk
- 1/2 cup cheddar cheese, shredded
- 1/2 cup frozen peas
- 1 tsp garlic powder
- Salt and pepper to taste

Instructions:

1. Preheat the oven to 350°F (175°C).
2. In a large bowl, mix together cooked chicken, rice, soup, milk, cheese, peas, garlic powder, salt, and pepper.
3. Transfer to a greased baking dish and cover with foil.
4. Bake for 30-40 minutes, or until heated through and the rice is tender.
5. Remove the foil, top with extra cheese, and bake for another 10 minutes.

Roasted Chicken with Herbs

Ingredients:

- 1 whole chicken (3-4 lbs)
- 4 cloves garlic, minced
- 1 tbsp rosemary, chopped
- 1 tbsp thyme, chopped
- 1 lemon, quartered
- 1/4 cup olive oil
- Salt and pepper to taste

Instructions:

1. Preheat the oven to 425°F (220°C).
2. Rub the chicken with olive oil, garlic, rosemary, thyme, salt, and pepper. Stuff the cavity with lemon quarters.
3. Place the chicken in a roasting pan and roast for 1-1.5 hours, or until the internal temperature reaches 165°F (75°C).
4. Let the chicken rest for 10 minutes before carving.

Eggplant Parmesan

Ingredients:

- 2 medium eggplants, sliced into 1/4-inch rounds
- 2 cups marinara sauce
- 2 cups mozzarella cheese, shredded
- 1/2 cup Parmesan cheese, grated
- 1 cup breadcrumbs
- 1/2 cup flour
- 2 eggs, beaten
- Olive oil for frying
- Salt and pepper to taste

Instructions:

1. Preheat the oven to 375°F (190°C).
2. Dredge eggplant slices in flour, dip in beaten eggs, and coat in breadcrumbs.
3. Heat olive oil in a pan and fry the eggplant slices until golden on both sides.
4. In a baking dish, layer fried eggplant, marinara sauce, mozzarella, and Parmesan. Repeat the layers.
5. Bake for 25-30 minutes, until the cheese is melted and bubbly.

Stuffed Mushrooms

Ingredients:

- 12 large mushrooms, stems removed
- 1/2 cup cream cheese, softened
- 1/4 cup grated Parmesan cheese
- 1/4 cup breadcrumbs
- 2 tbsp fresh parsley, chopped
- 1 clove garlic, minced
- Salt and pepper to taste

Instructions:

1. Preheat the oven to 350°F (175°C).
2. In a bowl, mix together cream cheese, Parmesan, breadcrumbs, parsley, garlic, salt, and pepper.
3. Stuff the mushroom caps with the mixture and place them on a baking sheet.
4. Bake for 20 minutes, until golden and bubbly.

Grilled Cheese Sandwich

Ingredients:

- 2 slices of bread (your choice, like white or whole wheat)
- 2 tbsp butter, softened
- 2 slices of cheddar cheese (or your preferred cheese)

Instructions:

1. Butter one side of each slice of bread.
2. Place a slice of cheese between the unbuttered sides of the bread.
3. Heat a skillet over medium heat. Once hot, add the sandwich, buttered side down.
4. Cook for 3-4 minutes until golden brown, then flip and cook the other side until the cheese is melted and the bread is golden.
5. Serve warm.

Butternut Squash Risotto

Ingredients:

- 1 small butternut squash, peeled, seeded, and cubed
- 2 tbsp olive oil
- 1 medium onion, chopped
- 2 cloves garlic, minced
- 1 1/2 cups Arborio rice
- 1/2 cup white wine (optional)
- 4 cups vegetable broth, warmed
- 1/2 cup grated Parmesan cheese
- Salt and pepper to taste

Instructions:

1. Preheat oven to 400°F (200°C). Toss butternut squash with olive oil, salt, and pepper. Roast for 25-30 minutes until tender.
2. In a large skillet, sauté onion and garlic in olive oil over medium heat until soft.
3. Add Arborio rice and cook, stirring, for 2 minutes.
4. Add white wine (if using) and cook until absorbed.
5. Gradually add warmed broth, one ladle at a time, stirring constantly until absorbed before adding more. Continue until the rice is creamy and tender, about 18-20 minutes.
6. Stir in roasted butternut squash and Parmesan cheese. Season with salt and pepper to taste.

Chicken Noodle Soup

Ingredients:

- 2 tbsp olive oil
- 1 medium onion, chopped
- 2 carrots, sliced
- 2 celery stalks, chopped
- 2 cloves garlic, minced
- 6 cups chicken broth
- 1 1/2 cups cooked chicken, shredded
- 1 1/2 cups egg noodles
- 1 tsp thyme
- Salt and pepper to taste

Instructions:

1. In a large pot, heat olive oil and sauté onion, carrots, and celery until softened, about 5 minutes.
2. Add garlic and cook for 1 more minute.
3. Pour in the chicken broth, bring to a boil, then reduce heat and simmer for 10 minutes.
4. Add cooked chicken, noodles, thyme, salt, and pepper. Simmer until noodles are tender, about 8-10 minutes.
5. Serve warm.

Cinnamon Rolls

Ingredients:

- 1 package active dry yeast
- 1/4 cup warm water
- 1/2 cup milk
- 1/2 cup butter, melted
- 1/4 cup sugar
- 1 tsp salt
- 2 1/2 cups all-purpose flour
- 1 egg
- 1/2 cup brown sugar
- 2 tsp cinnamon

Instructions:

1. In a small bowl, dissolve yeast in warm water and let it sit for 5-10 minutes.
2. In a large bowl, combine milk, butter, sugar, and salt. Add the yeast mixture, flour, and egg. Mix until dough forms.
3. Knead the dough for 5-7 minutes until smooth, then cover and let it rise for 1 hour.
4. Roll out the dough into a rectangle, spread butter, and sprinkle with brown sugar and cinnamon.
5. Roll the dough up and cut into 12 rolls. Place in a greased baking dish.
6. Bake at 375°F (190°C) for 20-25 minutes.

Sticky Toffee Pudding

Ingredients:

- 1 cup dates, chopped
- 1 tsp baking soda
- 1 cup boiling water
- 1/2 cup butter, softened
- 3/4 cup brown sugar
- 2 eggs
- 1 1/2 cups flour
- 1 tsp baking powder
- 1/2 tsp vanilla extract

For the Sauce:

- 1/2 cup butter
- 1/2 cup brown sugar
- 1/2 cup heavy cream

Instructions:

1. Preheat oven to 350°F (175°C). Grease a baking dish.
2. In a bowl, mix chopped dates and baking soda, then pour over boiling water. Let it sit for 10 minutes.
3. In a separate bowl, cream butter and sugar. Add eggs, flour, baking powder, and vanilla, mixing until smooth.
4. Stir in the date mixture and pour into the prepared dish. Bake for 30-35 minutes.

5. For the sauce, melt butter and brown sugar in a saucepan, then add cream and simmer for 5 minutes.

6. Serve the warm cake with sticky toffee sauce.

Baked Sweet Potatoes

Ingredients:

- 4 medium sweet potatoes
- Olive oil
- Salt and pepper

Instructions:

1. Preheat oven to 400°F (200°C).
2. Scrub the sweet potatoes and pierce each one a few times with a fork.
3. Rub with olive oil and sprinkle with salt and pepper.
4. Bake on a lined baking sheet for 45-60 minutes, until tender.
5. Serve with your favorite toppings, such as butter, brown sugar, or sour cream.

Mushroom Risotto

Ingredients:

- 1 cup Arborio rice
- 1/2 cup white wine
- 4 cups vegetable broth, warmed
- 1 tbsp olive oil
- 1 small onion, chopped
- 2 cups mushrooms, sliced
- 2 tbsp butter
- 1/2 cup Parmesan cheese
- Salt and pepper to taste

Instructions:

1. In a large pan, sauté onion in olive oil until softened. Add mushrooms and cook for 5 minutes until tender.
2. Add Arborio rice and cook, stirring for 2 minutes.
3. Pour in white wine and cook until absorbed.
4. Gradually add the warmed broth, one ladle at a time, stirring constantly until absorbed before adding more. Continue until rice is tender and creamy, about 18-20 minutes.
5. Stir in butter and Parmesan cheese. Season with salt and pepper.

Roasted Brussels Sprouts

Ingredients:

- 1 lb Brussels sprouts, trimmed and halved
- 2 tbsp olive oil
- Salt and pepper to taste

Instructions:

1. Preheat the oven to 400°F (200°C).
2. Toss Brussels sprouts with olive oil, salt, and pepper.
3. Spread them in a single layer on a baking sheet.
4. Roast for 20-25 minutes, shaking the pan halfway through, until crispy and golden brown.
5. Serve warm.

Salmon Chowder

Ingredients:

- 2 tbsp butter
- 1 small onion, chopped
- 2 cloves garlic, minced
- 3 cups vegetable or chicken broth
- 2 cups potatoes, diced
- 1 cup corn kernels (fresh or frozen)
- 1 lb salmon fillet, skin removed and diced
- 1 cup heavy cream
- Salt and pepper to taste

Instructions:

1. In a large pot, melt butter and sauté onion and garlic for 5 minutes.
2. Add broth, potatoes, and corn. Bring to a boil, then simmer for 10 minutes until potatoes are tender.
3. Add salmon and cook for 5-7 minutes, until it flakes easily with a fork.
4. Stir in heavy cream and season with salt and pepper.
5. Serve warm.

Warm Spinach and Bacon Salad

Ingredients:

- 4 cups fresh spinach leaves
- 4 slices bacon
- 1/2 red onion, thinly sliced
- 1/4 cup balsamic vinegar
- 1 tsp Dijon mustard
- 1 tsp honey
- 2 tbsp olive oil
- Salt and pepper to taste

Instructions:

1. Cook the bacon in a skillet over medium heat until crispy. Remove, crumble, and set aside.
2. In the same skillet, sauté the red onion in the bacon drippings for 2-3 minutes.
3. In a small bowl, whisk together balsamic vinegar, Dijon mustard, honey, olive oil, salt, and pepper.
4. In a large bowl, toss spinach with warm onions and the dressing.
5. Top with crumbled bacon and serve immediately.

Meatloaf

Ingredients:

- 1 lb ground beef
- 1/2 lb ground pork
- 1 onion, finely chopped
- 2 cloves garlic, minced
- 1/2 cup breadcrumbs
- 1/4 cup milk
- 1 egg
- 1/4 cup ketchup
- 1 tbsp Worcestershire sauce
- 1 tsp dried oregano
- Salt and pepper to taste
- 1/4 cup ketchup (for topping)

Instructions:

1. Preheat the oven to 375°F (190°C).
2. In a large bowl, combine ground beef, ground pork, onion, garlic, breadcrumbs, milk, egg, ketchup, Worcestershire sauce, oregano, salt, and pepper.
3. Form the mixture into a loaf and place it in a greased baking pan.
4. Spread ketchup on top of the meatloaf.
5. Bake for 45-50 minutes, until the meatloaf reaches an internal temperature of 160°F (71°C).

6. Let rest for 5 minutes before slicing and serving.

Potato Leek Soup

Ingredients:

- 2 tbsp butter
- 1 onion, chopped
- 2 leeks, cleaned and sliced
- 3 large potatoes, peeled and diced
- 4 cups vegetable or chicken broth
- 1 cup heavy cream
- Salt and pepper to taste
- Fresh parsley for garnish

Instructions:

1. In a large pot, melt butter over medium heat.
2. Add onion and leeks and cook until softened, about 5 minutes.
3. Add potatoes and broth, bringing the mixture to a boil. Reduce heat and simmer for 20 minutes, or until potatoes are tender.
4. Use an immersion blender to puree the soup until smooth.
5. Stir in heavy cream and season with salt and pepper.
6. Serve hot, garnished with fresh parsley.

Baked Apple Crisp

Ingredients:

- 5-6 apples, peeled, cored, and sliced
- 1/2 cup brown sugar
- 1 tsp cinnamon
- 1/2 tsp nutmeg
- 1/4 tsp salt
- 1/2 cup oats
- 1/2 cup all-purpose flour
- 1/4 cup butter, cold and cut into cubes
- 1/4 cup chopped pecans (optional)

Instructions:

1. Preheat oven to 350°F (175°C).
2. In a large bowl, toss apples with brown sugar, cinnamon, nutmeg, and salt. Transfer the mixture to a greased 9x9-inch baking dish.
3. In another bowl, combine oats, flour, butter, and pecans (if using). Use a pastry cutter or your fingers to blend the butter into the dry ingredients until the mixture resembles coarse crumbs.
4. Sprinkle the topping over the apples.
5. Bake for 35-40 minutes, until the apples are tender and the topping is golden brown.
6. Serve warm, with vanilla ice cream or whipped cream if desired.

Spiced Pear Tart

Ingredients:

- 1 sheet puff pastry, thawed
- 4 ripe pears, peeled and sliced
- 1/4 cup brown sugar
- 1 tsp cinnamon
- 1/4 tsp ginger
- 1/4 tsp nutmeg
- 1 tbsp butter, melted
- 1 tbsp honey

Instructions:

1. Preheat oven to 375°F (190°C).
2. Roll out the puff pastry on a baking sheet lined with parchment paper.
3. Arrange pear slices in a circular pattern over the pastry.
4. In a small bowl, mix brown sugar, cinnamon, ginger, and nutmeg. Sprinkle over the pears.
5. Drizzle melted butter and honey over the pears.
6. Bake for 25-30 minutes, or until the pastry is golden and the pears are tender.
7. Serve warm, optionally with a scoop of vanilla ice cream.

Lamb Stew

Ingredients:

- 1 lb lamb stew meat, cubed
- 2 tbsp olive oil
- 1 onion, chopped
- 3 carrots, peeled and sliced
- 3 potatoes, peeled and cubed
- 2 cloves garlic, minced
- 4 cups beef broth
- 1 tsp rosemary
- 1 tsp thyme
- Salt and pepper to taste

Instructions:

1. In a large pot, heat olive oil over medium heat. Brown the lamb in batches, then set aside.
2. In the same pot, sauté onion, carrots, and garlic until softened.
3. Add the lamb back to the pot, along with potatoes, broth, rosemary, thyme, salt, and pepper.
4. Bring to a boil, then reduce heat and simmer for 1 1/2 to 2 hours, until the lamb is tender.
5. Serve warm.

Chicken Alfredo

Ingredients:

- 2 tbsp olive oil
- 2 chicken breasts, sliced
- 2 cloves garlic, minced
- 1 cup heavy cream
- 1/2 cup grated Parmesan cheese
- 1 lb fettuccine pasta, cooked
- Salt and pepper to taste
- Fresh parsley for garnish

Instructions:

1. In a large skillet, heat olive oil over medium heat. Cook chicken until golden brown and cooked through. Set aside.
2. In the same skillet, sauté garlic for 1 minute, then add heavy cream and bring to a simmer.
3. Stir in Parmesan cheese and cook until the sauce thickens, about 3-5 minutes.
4. Toss the cooked pasta and chicken in the sauce, adding salt and pepper to taste.
5. Garnish with fresh parsley and serve immediately.

Cauliflower Gratin

Ingredients:

- 1 head cauliflower, broken into florets
- 2 tbsp butter
- 1/4 cup all-purpose flour
- 2 cups milk
- 1 cup grated Gruyère cheese
- Salt and pepper to taste

Instructions:

1. Preheat oven to 375°F (190°C).
2. Steam cauliflower florets until tender, about 10 minutes.
3. In a saucepan, melt butter over medium heat. Stir in flour and cook for 2 minutes.
4. Gradually whisk in milk and cook, stirring constantly, until thickened.
5. Stir in cheese, salt, and pepper.
6. In a baking dish, combine cauliflower and cheese sauce.
7. Bake for 20-25 minutes until bubbly and golden.
8. Serve warm.

Pulled Pork Sandwiches

Ingredients:

- 3-4 lbs pork shoulder
- 1 onion, sliced
- 2 cloves garlic, minced
- 1 cup BBQ sauce
- 1 tbsp apple cider vinegar
- 1 tsp paprika
- Salt and pepper to taste
- Burger buns

Instructions:

1. In a slow cooker, combine pork shoulder, onion, garlic, BBQ sauce, vinegar, paprika, salt, and pepper.
2. Cook on low for 8 hours or high for 4-5 hours, until the pork is tender and easily shredded.
3. Shred the pork using two forks and toss with the sauce.
4. Serve on burger buns with additional BBQ sauce if desired.

Warm Spinach and Bacon Salad

Ingredients:

- 4 cups fresh spinach leaves
- 4 slices bacon
- 1/2 red onion, thinly sliced
- 1/4 cup balsamic vinegar
- 1 tsp Dijon mustard
- 1 tsp honey
- 2 tbsp olive oil
- Salt and pepper to taste

Instructions:

1. Cook the bacon in a skillet over medium heat until crispy. Remove, crumble, and set aside.
2. In the same skillet, sauté the red onion in the bacon drippings for 2-3 minutes.
3. In a small bowl, whisk together balsamic vinegar, Dijon mustard, honey, olive oil, salt, and pepper.
4. In a large bowl, toss spinach with warm onions and the dressing.
5. Top with crumbled bacon and serve immediately.

Meatloaf

Ingredients:

- 1 lb ground beef
- 1/2 lb ground pork
- 1 onion, finely chopped
- 2 cloves garlic, minced
- 1/2 cup breadcrumbs
- 1/4 cup milk
- 1 egg
- 1/4 cup ketchup
- 1 tbsp Worcestershire sauce
- 1 tsp dried oregano
- Salt and pepper to taste
- 1/4 cup ketchup (for topping)

Instructions:

1. Preheat the oven to 375°F (190°C).
2. In a large bowl, combine ground beef, ground pork, onion, garlic, breadcrumbs, milk, egg, ketchup, Worcestershire sauce, oregano, salt, and pepper.
3. Form the mixture into a loaf and place it in a greased baking pan.
4. Spread ketchup on top of the meatloaf.
5. Bake for 45-50 minutes, until the meatloaf reaches an internal temperature of 160°F (71°C).

6. Let rest for 5 minutes before slicing and serving.

Potato Leek Soup

Ingredients:

- 2 tbsp butter
- 1 onion, chopped
- 2 leeks, cleaned and sliced
- 3 large potatoes, peeled and diced
- 4 cups vegetable or chicken broth
- 1 cup heavy cream
- Salt and pepper to taste
- Fresh parsley for garnish

Instructions:

1. In a large pot, melt butter over medium heat.
2. Add onion and leeks and cook until softened, about 5 minutes.
3. Add potatoes and broth, bringing the mixture to a boil. Reduce heat and simmer for 20 minutes, or until potatoes are tender.
4. Use an immersion blender to puree the soup until smooth.
5. Stir in heavy cream and season with salt and pepper.
6. Serve hot, garnished with fresh parsley.

Baked Apple Crisp

Ingredients:

- 5-6 apples, peeled, cored, and sliced
- 1/2 cup brown sugar
- 1 tsp cinnamon
- 1/2 tsp nutmeg
- 1/4 tsp salt
- 1/2 cup oats
- 1/2 cup all-purpose flour
- 1/4 cup butter, cold and cut into cubes
- 1/4 cup chopped pecans (optional)

Instructions:

1. Preheat oven to 350°F (175°C).
2. In a large bowl, toss apples with brown sugar, cinnamon, nutmeg, and salt. Transfer the mixture to a greased 9x9-inch baking dish.
3. In another bowl, combine oats, flour, butter, and pecans (if using). Use a pastry cutter or your fingers to blend the butter into the dry ingredients until the mixture resembles coarse crumbs.
4. Sprinkle the topping over the apples.
5. Bake for 35-40 minutes, until the apples are tender and the topping is golden brown.
6. Serve warm, with vanilla ice cream or whipped cream if desired.

Spiced Pear Tart

Ingredients:

- 1 sheet puff pastry, thawed
- 4 ripe pears, peeled and sliced
- 1/4 cup brown sugar
- 1 tsp cinnamon
- 1/4 tsp ginger
- 1/4 tsp nutmeg
- 1 tbsp butter, melted
- 1 tbsp honey

Instructions:

1. Preheat oven to 375°F (190°C).
2. Roll out the puff pastry on a baking sheet lined with parchment paper.
3. Arrange pear slices in a circular pattern over the pastry.
4. In a small bowl, mix brown sugar, cinnamon, ginger, and nutmeg. Sprinkle over the pears.
5. Drizzle melted butter and honey over the pears.
6. Bake for 25-30 minutes, or until the pastry is golden and the pears are tender.
7. Serve warm, optionally with a scoop of vanilla ice cream.

Lamb Stew

Ingredients:

- 1 lb lamb stew meat, cubed
- 2 tbsp olive oil
- 1 onion, chopped
- 3 carrots, peeled and sliced
- 3 potatoes, peeled and cubed
- 2 cloves garlic, minced
- 4 cups beef broth
- 1 tsp rosemary
- 1 tsp thyme
- Salt and pepper to taste

Instructions:

1. In a large pot, heat olive oil over medium heat. Brown the lamb in batches, then set aside.
2. In the same pot, sauté onion, carrots, and garlic until softened.
3. Add the lamb back to the pot, along with potatoes, broth, rosemary, thyme, salt, and pepper.
4. Bring to a boil, then reduce heat and simmer for 1 1/2 to 2 hours, until the lamb is tender.
5. Serve warm.

Chicken Alfredo

Ingredients:

- 2 tbsp olive oil
- 2 chicken breasts, sliced
- 2 cloves garlic, minced
- 1 cup heavy cream
- 1/2 cup grated Parmesan cheese
- 1 lb fettuccine pasta, cooked
- Salt and pepper to taste
- Fresh parsley for garnish

Instructions:

1. In a large skillet, heat olive oil over medium heat. Cook chicken until golden brown and cooked through. Set aside.
2. In the same skillet, sauté garlic for 1 minute, then add heavy cream and bring to a simmer.
3. Stir in Parmesan cheese and cook until the sauce thickens, about 3-5 minutes.
4. Toss the cooked pasta and chicken in the sauce, adding salt and pepper to taste.
5. Garnish with fresh parsley and serve immediately.

Cauliflower Gratin

Ingredients:

- 1 head cauliflower, broken into florets
- 2 tbsp butter
- 1/4 cup all-purpose flour
- 2 cups milk
- 1 cup grated Gruyère cheese
- Salt and pepper to taste

Instructions:

1. Preheat oven to 375°F (190°C).
2. Steam cauliflower florets until tender, about 10 minutes.
3. In a saucepan, melt butter over medium heat. Stir in flour and cook for 2 minutes.
4. Gradually whisk in milk and cook, stirring constantly, until thickened.
5. Stir in cheese, salt, and pepper.
6. In a baking dish, combine cauliflower and cheese sauce.
7. Bake for 20-25 minutes until bubbly and golden.
8. Serve warm.

Pulled Pork Sandwiches

Ingredients:

- 3-4 lbs pork shoulder
- 1 onion, sliced
- 2 cloves garlic, minced
- 1 cup BBQ sauce
- 1 tbsp apple cider vinegar
- 1 tsp paprika
- Salt and pepper to taste
- Burger buns

Instructions:

1. In a slow cooker, combine pork shoulder, onion, garlic, BBQ sauce, vinegar, paprika, salt, and pepper.
2. Cook on low for 8 hours or high for 4-5 hours, until the pork is tender and easily shredded.
3. Shred the pork using two forks and toss with the sauce.
4. Serve on burger buns with additional BBQ sauce if desired.

Risotto with Winter Greens

Ingredients:

- 1 tbsp olive oil
- 1 small onion, finely chopped
- 2 cloves garlic, minced
- 1 cup Arborio rice
- 4 cups vegetable or chicken broth
- 1/2 cup dry white wine
- 1 bunch kale or Swiss chard, chopped
- 1/2 cup grated Parmesan cheese
- Salt and pepper to taste

Instructions:

1. In a large saucepan, heat olive oil over medium heat.
2. Add onion and garlic, cooking until softened, about 3-4 minutes.
3. Stir in Arborio rice and cook for 1-2 minutes until lightly toasted.
4. Add wine and cook until absorbed.
5. Gradually add broth, 1/2 cup at a time, stirring continuously until liquid is absorbed before adding more. Continue until rice is tender, about 18-20 minutes.
6. Stir in winter greens and cook for an additional 3-4 minutes until wilted.
7. Remove from heat and stir in Parmesan cheese.
8. Season with salt and pepper to taste, and serve warm.

Potato Gratin

Ingredients:

- 2 lbs potatoes, peeled and thinly sliced
- 2 cups heavy cream
- 1 cup grated Gruyère cheese
- 1 clove garlic, minced
- 1 tsp fresh thyme
- Salt and pepper to taste
- 2 tbsp butter (for greasing the pan)

Instructions:

1. Preheat oven to 375°F (190°C).
2. Grease a 9x13-inch baking dish with butter.
3. Layer the sliced potatoes in the dish, seasoning each layer with garlic, thyme, salt, and pepper.
4. Pour the heavy cream over the potatoes.
5. Sprinkle the grated Gruyère cheese evenly over the top.
6. Cover with foil and bake for 45 minutes.
7. Remove foil and bake for an additional 20-25 minutes, until the top is golden and bubbly.
8. Let cool for 5 minutes before serving.

Lemon Bread Pudding

Ingredients:

- 4 cups cubed day-old bread
- 2 cups milk
- 1/2 cup sugar
- 4 large eggs
- 1 tbsp lemon zest
- 1/4 cup fresh lemon juice
- 1/2 tsp vanilla extract
- 1/4 tsp cinnamon
- Powdered sugar for dusting (optional)

Instructions:

1. Preheat oven to 350°F (175°C).
2. In a large bowl, whisk together milk, sugar, eggs, lemon zest, lemon juice, vanilla, and cinnamon.
3. Add cubed bread and stir to combine. Let it sit for 10 minutes to allow the bread to soak.
4. Pour the mixture into a greased 9x9-inch baking dish.
5. Bake for 35-40 minutes, or until the top is golden and a toothpick comes out clean.
6. Dust with powdered sugar before serving, if desired.

Apple and Cranberry Sauce

Ingredients:

- 2 apples, peeled, cored, and diced
- 1 cup fresh cranberries
- 1/2 cup sugar
- 1/4 cup water
- 1/2 tsp cinnamon
- 1/4 tsp nutmeg
- 1 tbsp lemon juice

Instructions:

1. In a medium saucepan, combine apples, cranberries, sugar, water, cinnamon, nutmeg, and lemon juice.
2. Bring to a boil, then reduce heat and simmer for 15-20 minutes, stirring occasionally, until the fruit breaks down and the sauce thickens.
3. Remove from heat and let cool before serving.

Mulled Wine

Ingredients:

- 1 bottle red wine (750 ml)
- 1 orange, sliced
- 1 lemon, sliced
- 4 whole cloves
- 2 cinnamon sticks
- 1/4 cup honey or sugar (to taste)
- 1 star anise (optional)

Instructions:

1. In a large pot, combine the wine, orange slices, lemon slices, cloves, cinnamon sticks, honey, and star anise.
2. Heat over medium-low heat until warm, but not boiling.
3. Simmer for 15-20 minutes to allow the flavors to meld.
4. Remove from heat and strain before serving.
5. Serve warm in mugs or heatproof glasses.

Goulash

Ingredients:

- 1 lb beef stew meat, cubed
- 2 tbsp olive oil
- 1 onion, chopped
- 2 cloves garlic, minced
- 1 red bell pepper, chopped
- 1 can (14.5 oz) diced tomatoes
- 2 tbsp paprika
- 1 tsp thyme
- 1/2 cup beef broth
- Salt and pepper to taste
- Cooked egg noodles (for serving)

Instructions:

1. In a large pot, heat olive oil over medium heat. Brown the beef in batches, then set aside.
2. In the same pot, sauté onion, garlic, and red bell pepper until softened.
3. Stir in paprika and thyme, then add diced tomatoes and beef broth.
4. Return the beef to the pot and bring to a boil.
5. Reduce heat, cover, and simmer for 1 1/2 to 2 hours, until the beef is tender.
6. Season with salt and pepper to taste.
7. Serve over cooked egg noodles.

Baked Brie with Jam

Ingredients:

- 1 wheel of Brie cheese (8 oz)
- 1/4 cup fruit jam (apricot, raspberry, or fig)
- 1 sheet puff pastry
- 1 egg (for egg wash)

Instructions:

1. Preheat oven to 375°F (190°C).
2. Unwrap the Brie and place it on a sheet of puff pastry.
3. Spread the fruit jam on top of the Brie.
4. Fold the puff pastry over the Brie, sealing the edges.
5. Brush the pastry with a beaten egg.
6. Bake for 20-25 minutes, until the pastry is golden and puffed.
7. Serve with crackers or sliced baguette.

Chocolate Lava Cake

Ingredients:

- 1/2 cup unsalted butter
- 6 oz semisweet chocolate, chopped
- 1/2 cup powdered sugar
- 2 large eggs
- 2 egg yolks
- 1/4 cup all-purpose flour
- 1/4 tsp vanilla extract
- Pinch of salt
- Vanilla ice cream or whipped cream (for serving)

Instructions:

1. Preheat oven to 425°F (220°C). Grease 4 ramekins with butter and dust with cocoa powder.
2. In a microwave-safe bowl, melt butter and chocolate together in 30-second intervals, stirring in between.
3. Stir in powdered sugar, eggs, egg yolks, flour, vanilla, and salt.
4. Pour the batter evenly into the prepared ramekins.
5. Bake for 12-14 minutes, until the edges are set but the center is soft.
6. Let the cakes cool for 1 minute, then carefully invert onto plates.
7. Serve with vanilla ice cream or whipped cream.

Eggnog

Ingredients:

- 4 large eggs
- 1/2 cup sugar
- 2 cups whole milk
- 1 cup heavy cream
- 1/2 cup bourbon or rum (optional)
- 1 tsp vanilla extract
- Freshly grated nutmeg (for garnish)

Instructions:

1. In a medium bowl, whisk together eggs and sugar until pale and thick.
2. In a saucepan, heat milk and heavy cream over medium heat until just simmering.
3. Gradually whisk the hot milk mixture into the egg mixture.
4. Return the mixture to the saucepan and cook over low heat, stirring constantly, until it thickens slightly.
5. Remove from heat and stir in the bourbon or rum (if using) and vanilla extract.
6. Chill the eggnog in the refrigerator for at least 2 hours before serving.
7. Garnish with freshly grated nutmeg.

Roasted Chestnuts

Ingredients:

- 1 lb fresh chestnuts
- Water
- Salt (optional)

Instructions:

1. Preheat your oven to 425°F (220°C).
2. Using a sharp knife, make a small "X" on the flat side of each chestnut to prevent them from exploding during roasting.
3. Place chestnuts in a large pot, cover with water, and bring to a boil. Let them simmer for 5 minutes.
4. Drain chestnuts and spread them on a baking sheet.
5. Roast in the oven for 20-25 minutes, shaking the pan occasionally, until the shells peel back and the nut is tender.
6. Remove from oven and allow to cool slightly. Peel the shells while the chestnuts are still warm.
7. Serve warm, optionally sprinkling with a pinch of salt.

Caramelized Onion Soup

Ingredients:

- 3 large onions, thinly sliced
- 2 tbsp olive oil
- 1 tbsp butter
- 4 cups beef or vegetable broth
- 1/2 cup dry white wine (optional)
- 1 tsp thyme
- 1 tbsp sugar
- Salt and pepper to taste
- French baguette slices (for serving)
- 1 cup grated Gruyère or Swiss cheese (for topping)

Instructions:

1. In a large pot, heat olive oil and butter over medium heat.
2. Add onions and cook, stirring occasionally, for about 30-40 minutes until the onions are golden brown and caramelized.
3. Sprinkle sugar over the onions and cook for another 5 minutes to enhance the caramelization.
4. Add wine (if using), scraping any browned bits off the bottom of the pot.
5. Pour in the broth, add thyme, and bring to a simmer. Cook for 15-20 minutes to allow the flavors to meld.
6. Season with salt and pepper to taste.

7. Toast the baguette slices, then top with cheese and place under the broiler until melted and bubbly.

8. Serve the soup with the cheesy toast on top.

Pumpkin Bread

Ingredients:

- 1 3/4 cups all-purpose flour
- 1 tsp baking soda
- 1/2 tsp baking powder
- 1/2 tsp salt
- 1 tsp cinnamon
- 1/2 tsp nutmeg
- 1/4 tsp ground ginger
- 1/4 tsp ground cloves
- 1/2 cup sugar
- 1/2 cup brown sugar
- 2 large eggs
- 1 cup pumpkin puree
- 1/2 cup vegetable oil
- 1/4 cup milk
- 1 tsp vanilla extract

Instructions:

1. Preheat the oven to 350°F (175°C). Grease a 9x5-inch loaf pan.
2. In a medium bowl, whisk together flour, baking soda, baking powder, salt, and spices.
3. In a separate large bowl, beat together sugars, eggs, pumpkin puree, oil, milk, and vanilla extract.

4. Gradually add the dry ingredients to the wet ingredients, mixing until combined.

5. Pour the batter into the prepared loaf pan and smooth the top.

6. Bake for 60-70 minutes, or until a toothpick comes out clean.

7. Let the bread cool in the pan for 10 minutes, then transfer to a wire rack to cool completely.

Snowball Cookies

Ingredients:

- 1 cup unsalted butter, softened
- 1/4 cup powdered sugar
- 1 tsp vanilla extract
- 2 cups all-purpose flour
- 1/2 cup finely chopped walnuts (optional)
- Powdered sugar (for rolling)

Instructions:

1. Preheat the oven to 350°F (175°C). Line a baking sheet with parchment paper.
2. In a large bowl, cream together the butter and powdered sugar until light and fluffy.
3. Add the vanilla extract and flour, mixing until just combined. Stir in walnuts, if using.
4. Roll the dough into small 1-inch balls and place them on the prepared baking sheet.
5. Bake for 12-15 minutes, or until the bottoms are lightly golden.
6. While still warm, roll the cookies in powdered sugar to coat.
7. Allow to cool completely before serving.